HAPPY NEW

Written by Helen Ch

D0715241

Contents

Collins

Let's celebrate!

On New Year's Eve, we say goodbye to the old year and hello to the new one. Many **traditions** from the past are still part of our celebrations today.

Australia

Sydney

Fireworks light up
Sydney Harbour.

Turning over a new leaf

For many years, people have made promises to be good or to break a bad habit. These are called New Year's resolutions.

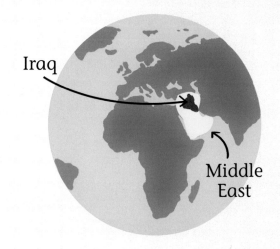

Iraq

Middle East

This **carving** from 2,300 BCE shows this resolution was to give a borrowed tool back to its owner.

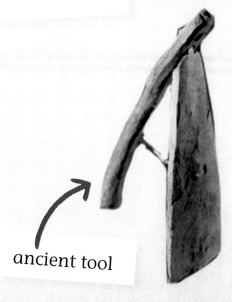

ancient tool

Giving gifts

Since **ancient** times, people have greeted each other with a gift.

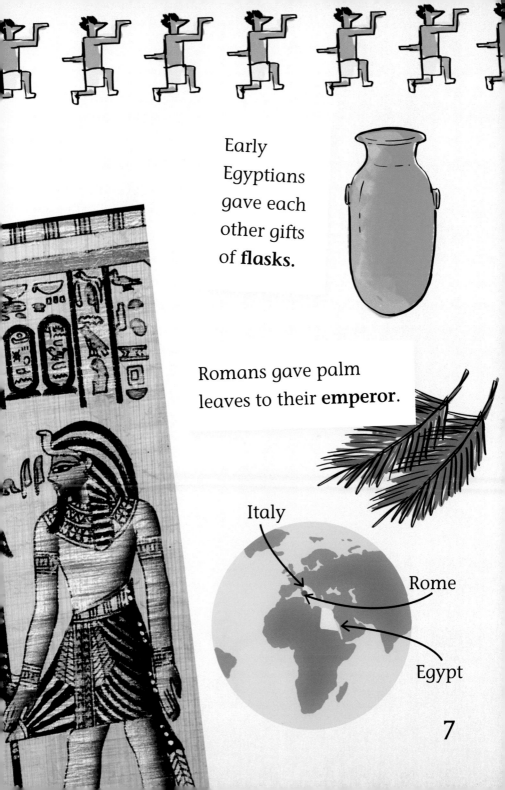

Early Egyptians gave each other gifts of **flasks**.

Romans gave palm leaves to their **emperor**.

Italy

Rome

Egypt

Eating lucky food

A **custom** in Belgium and Holland since 1682 is to bake and eat special round treats to bring good luck.

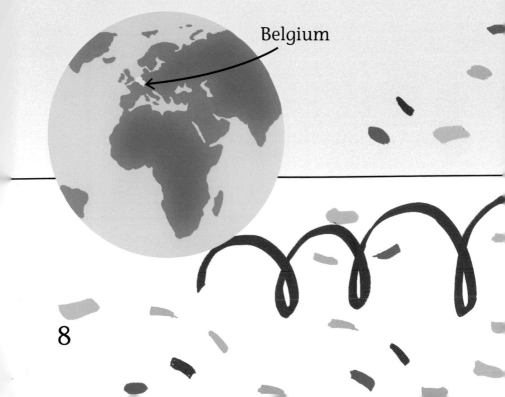

Belgium

Oliebollen are lucky doughnuts!

9

Dancing dragons and firecrackers

Chinese dragons **weave** and dance through the streets. Dragons are a **symbol** of China and bring good luck.

People also light
firecrackers to
bring good luck.

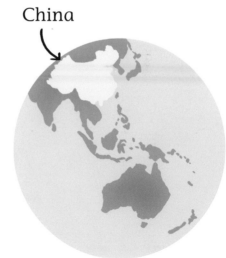

China

Chinese New Year

Chinese New Year happens in January or February.
In China, each year is shown by a different animal.

China

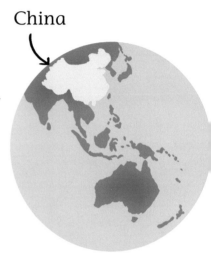

year of the
sheep

year of the
monkey

year of the
rooster

year of the
dragon

year of the
horse

year of the
snake

year of the
rabbit

year of the
tiger

year of the
ox

year of the
dog

year of the
pig

year of the
rat

Singing in the New Year

A Scottish song called "Auld Lang Syne" reminds people not to forget their old friends. People have sung this song since 1788!

Scotland

Making noise

Floats and marching bands make this parade a New Year tradition with families.

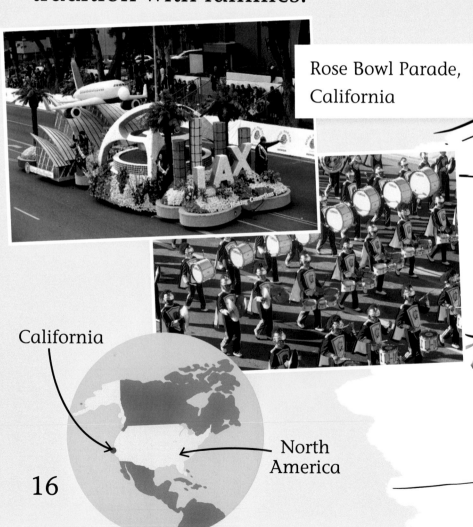

Rose Bowl Parade, California

California

North America

In South Africa, everyone enjoys the music at carnival time.

Cape Town

South Africa

Kaapse Klopse, Cape Town

Watching fireworks

Exploding fireworks colour the night sky all around the world.

London

New York

COW

RIO DE JANE

Venice

Party time!

The New Year is a time to celebrate with friends and family.

From India ...

... to Antarctica.

Happy New Year!

Glossary

ancient   very old

carving   a design cut into stone or wood

custom   a traditional way of behaving

emperor   a male ruler of an empire

flasks   rounded bottles with a narrow neck

symbol   a character used to stand for
                 an object

traditions   beliefs and customs handed down
                 over many years

weave   to wind from side to side

New Year's Eve around the world

North America

Scotland

South America

Belgium

China

Egypt

South
Africa

Australia

23

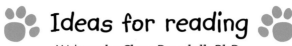

Ideas for reading

Written by Clare Dowdall, PhD
Lecturer and Primary Literacy Consultant

Learning objectives: to read words containing taught GPCs and –s, –es, –ing, –ed, –er and –est endings; link what children read or hear to their own experiences; check that the text makes sense to them as they read and correct inaccurate reading; give well-structured descriptions and explanations

Curriculum links: geography

High frequency words: the, are, our, many, people, was, their, other, also, friends, everyone

Interest words: carving, resolution, ancient, Romans, emperor, Egyptians, flasks, custom, weave, symbol, tradition

Word count: 242

Resources: pens and paper, images of New Year celebrations, globe, map of the world

Getting started

- Look at the front and back covers. Read the title and blurb. Ask children to describe how they celebrate New Year in their family.

- Ask children to describe how they think New Year might be celebrated in different countries around the world.

- Read the contents together, looking for words with the "ing" ending.

Reading and responding

- Turn to pp 2–3. Ask children to read the title. Help them to use known phonic strategies and to break the word "celebrate" into syllables (*cel-e-brate*). Discuss what it means, and why it has an exclamation mark at the end.